A Choice for Sarah

Story by Sonny Mulheron
Illustrations by Julia Crouth

"I have to learn a new piece for my violin recital," said Sarah, when she came in from her music lesson. "I've only got five weeks to get it right, Mom. It sounded great when Mr. Kahn played it, but I think it might be too hard for me."

Mom smiled at her. "I'm sure you'll be able to do it," she said. "Why don't you practice it now? I love listening to you play."

Sarah started to play her new piece, but she kept making mistakes. "I'll never get it right," she said. She put her violin away and ran outside to practice handstands for her gym class instead.

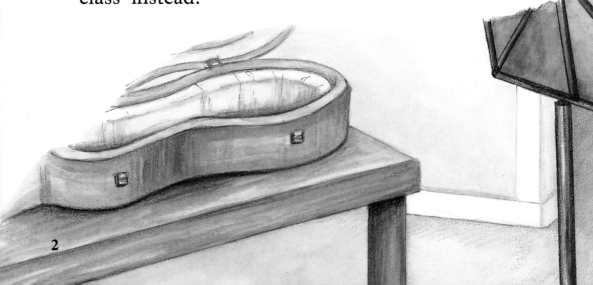

At gym the next afternoon, the children began with floor exercises: handstands, forward rolls, backward rolls, cartwheels, and split leaps.

At the end of the class, everyone gathered around Mandy, their coach. "We've got a good chance of doing well in the next competition," she told them. "It's in five weeks' time. I'd like all of you to practice as much as possible. I want everyone to do their best."

"How am I going to practice my gym, and the violin, and do all my school work as well?" thought Sarah.

5

At her next violin lesson, Mr. Kahn asked Sarah to try the new piece he had given her. She began, but she couldn't play it right.

"Oh," she said. "That sounded awful!"

Mr. Kahn was surprised. "You usually play better than that, Sarah! Would you like to try it again?" he suggested.

But Sarah still couldn't get it right. "I didn't have enough time to practice," she explained. "I have to work hard for a gym competition, too. It's on Saturday, the first of March."

"But that's the same day as your music recital!" said Mr. Kahn.

"Is it?" said Sarah. "What am I going to do?"

"I'm afraid you won't be able to do both," said Mr. Kahn. "You'll have to make a choice."

"But I love doing gym. I like it just as much as playing the violin," said Sarah.

"Well, you'll have to make up your mind soon," said Mr. Kahn. "Why don't you talk about it with your parents?"

But talking about it didn't help much. Sarah still couldn't decide. The next time she had a gym class, she told Mandy that her music recital was on the same day as the competition.

"I don't know what to do!" exclaimed Sarah.

Mandy looked thoughtful. "Well, if you are going to be in the gym competition, you will have to practice just like everyone else," she said.

"But I'll need to practice for my violin recital, too," said Sarah.

"I understand your problem, Sarah," said Mandy, "but you are going to have to make a decision. Think about it and let me know as soon as you can."

That evening, Sarah and her mom watched some champion gymnasts on television. They all had perfect timing and amazing balance.

"I'd love to be able to do split leaps the way that girl does," said Sarah. "If I keep practicing, do you think I could be as good as she is?"

"Perhaps," said Mom. "Isn't she fantastic! But to be that good you would have to practice for hours every day."

Sarah sighed. What was she going to do?

The following weekend, Sarah's parents took her to the town hall to hear a visiting orchestra. It was exciting to hear so many instruments playing together, and to be sitting so close to the musicians.

The sound of the violins soared above the rest of the instruments. Sarah forgot everything else as she listened to the music. She had never heard anything quite so beautiful before.

After the concert, Sarah said to her parents, "I loved the sound of those violins so much. I know what I'm going to do now. I'm going to work hard for my violin recital."

"I'm glad you've made your decision," said Sarah's dad.

"So am I," said Sarah, "and now I can tell Mandy that I've decided not to be in the gym competition."

Sarah felt relieved that she had finally made a choice.

The next day, Sarah picked up her violin again. She practiced every day, and by the end of the week she could play her new piece right through without stopping.

15

"That sounded great!" said Mr. Kahn, when Sarah played it to him. "You must have worked so hard!"

"I have," said Sarah. "I want to do well in the recital because, one day, I'd like to play the violin in a big orchestra."